FRIENDS IN BUSINESS

THE BLUEPRINT FOR DOING BUSINESS WITH FAMILY AND FRIENDS

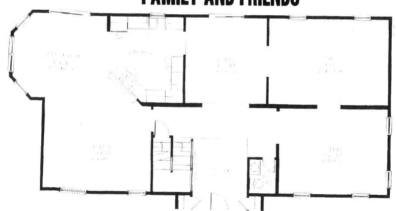

**AUTHORS: RENELDO RANDALL, MBA
& PJ PIGGOTT, BS**

RPEO Publishing

DEDICATION

We are dedicating this book to William H. Moore Jr. He is one of our closest friends and is the person responsible for introducing us.

ACKNOWLEDGEMENTS

Our thanks go to our parents, who have always believed in us. I (Reneldo) would like to thank my wife Ashley for allowing me to be ambitious and giving me the freedom to work. We would also like to thank our circle of friends, partners, and supporters.

TABLE OF CONTENTS

"The beginning is the most important part of the work"
- Plato

WHY WE ARE WRITING THIS BOOK?

We are writing this book because we have been successful at working together on teams, in businesses, and in organizations assisting them to run proficiently, expand and grow for nearly 30 years. What we have been able to accomplish from the outside looking in appears to happen fairly naturally, and components of it do, but the magic that we showcase is due in large part and is birthed out of the fact that we have been like-minded friends for years. We have thousands of hours of practice working through situations and getting to know one another spanning from middle school, through college, through our early professional lives. It is this level of exposure to each other that enables us not to have to force synergy or energy onto one another. This process has become involuntary and ultimately allows us to get things done more efficiently and effectively than most.

Why is it that the advice that is often given to individuals that endeavor to do business with family and/or friends is that it is not a good idea? When polled and asked, "Why don't people do business with friends and family?", here are a few of the responses that we received.

"Doing business with family is most of the time disappointing they don't always see the vision or the end goal…"

"Fear of disappointment. Feeling it would not be worth losing the friendship."

"Friends have an unfair expectation of special privilege…"

"Friends do not always respect your professionalism, subject matter expertise, and business-based decisions."

"Money can cause things to go wrong."

Do not be fooled, there are successful friends in commerce. A few popular ones are Ben and Jerry, Hewlett and Packard and even Starbucks was started by friends. However, there still seems to be a dark cloud over the idea of going into business with friends and family. We are here to fill that gap as we are confident that we have developed a blueprint for how friends and/or family can successfully conduct business together over long periods and change this conventional idea that family and/or friends cannot successfully run an enterprise together.

WHY WRITE THIS BOOK NOW?

PJ and I feel this book is worth writing because this issue, of doing business with family or friends, has been a topic of discussion and unresolved contemplation for decades. A topic and concept that you would think should not be as difficult to understand and move forward with. I mean, how hard can it be? Friends and family should be able to conduct business together without issue, right?

If they cannot or have not been able to as naturally or seamlessly as us or those that came before us have, that is understandable because all relationships are different, take work and take time. However, for those who struggle with this concept or who need to be introduced to this concept before entering a Friend/Family enterprise, this book is their opportunity to receive the blueprint on how to conduct business with Family/Friends successfully while maintaining and even strengthening the relationship.

Who better to spend time with, make money with and then spend money with than your family/friends? Entrepreneurship has become a trendy and sexy topic. People like what the word represents, at its best, freedom and wealth. However, many people are not born entrepreneurs – that is if an entrepreneur can even be born, they want the perceived lifestyle and accompanying respect that they envision that is attached to entrepreneurship. Pursuing entrepreneurship and doing business alone is one thing, but adding pursuing that aspiration with others and creating a partnership particularly with loved ones creates a unique set of circumstances that requires a certain mode of thinking and development of skills both of which can be acquired by the proper proactive planning and tooling. Now that you are reading this book, there are a few other books we would recommend to assist with your mode of thinking (mindset) and your development of skills (skill set). Please note that there are many other outstanding books out there and this is by no means an exhaustive list but a few that have been useful for us and fit the theme of this book.

MINDSET

Think and Grow Rich | Author: Napoleon Hill

Rich Dad Poor Dad | Author: Robert T. Kiyosaki

7 Habits of Highly Successful People | Author: Steven Covey

Teammates Matter | Author: Alan Williams

When You Want to Succeed as Bad as You Want to Breathe
| Author: Dr. Eric Thomas

SKILLSET

How to Win Friends and Influence People | Author: Dale Carnegie

Real Leadership: 9 Simple Practices for Leading and Loving with Purpose | Author: John Addison

The Personal MBA | Author: Josh Kaufman

Crushing It! | Author: Gary Vaynerchuk

The 4-Hour Workweek | Author: Timothy Ferriss

There is a growing number of entrepreneurs whose transition into entrepreneurship is situational. You rarely hear of a business of any significance that was started by or run by one individual, so entrepreneurs regardless of whether they are born entrepreneurs or made entrepreneurs are looking for partners. We are in, at the time of the writing of this book, what is being called the "gig economy" (I am sure they will come up with other catchy names in the future). As an aftermath of the great recession and as a result of new technologies and robotics we have seen unprecedented amounts of company: downsizing, rightsizing, restructuring, corporate closings, corporate acquisitions and government shutdowns. All these terms simply mean that someone lost or is at risk of losing their job. Thus, people do not feel as secure in their jobs as they once did. They are looking for alternatives for securing a second source of income. In an economy with this type of unparalleled job shrinkage, another job does not feel as secure. Hence, the rise of the "gig economy." When most people think about getting into something new, be it business or otherwise, they naturally and typically consult the individuals closest to them who end up being their family and friends. They hope and expect these loved ones to support them in at least one of three ways 1) as a business partner 2) as a business investor or 3) as a customer.

WHAT'S IN THE BOOK?

If any of this intrigues you, let us explain to you in short how we intend on revealing these friends/family in business secrets in this blueprint. We will first provide you context to the layers of our friendship. Then we will go through the process of how to determine if the friend or family member you are considering will be a good business partner. We discuss casting and agreeing on a vision and strategically planning how you might scale the business in the future. Note: this is a continuous conversation. Then we will address some of the common issues that occur when family members and friends do business together. This book aims to provide tools for how to proactively address those issues or how to deal with those issues if they are currently happening. The power and importance of purposeful, honest and consistent…consistent communication and yes, I meant to put consistent 2, now 3 times because it is that important! The use of electronic and digital mediums to communicate with your business partners allows you to keep this level of consistent communication ongoing – especially with people being busy juggling multiple tasks and priorities.

THE AUTHORS' UNIQUE RELATIONSHIP

We have been best friends since 1993. Although we had seen each other on a few occasions we did not officially meet or know each other until the summer before entering our 7th grade year of middle school. We were 13 years old. My (Reneldo's) family moved to the area of Williamsburg, VA where PJ lived, at that time. Our first introduction came by way of a mutual friend William Moore Jr.

It was the summer of 1993. William and I would get together to do what 13-year-old boys do - play basketball, video games and go swimming - and we would stop by PJ's house. PJ would be home, but he never answered the door – we could see him peeking through the blinds. We figured PJ's mother told him not to open the door when she was not home. After knowing her for almost 30 years, that was likely the instruction she gave PJ.

Fast forward a few months to the first day of 7th grade. I was starting a new school and PJ and I rode the same bus. We were not in the same classes but both of us played football and on the football field at Toano Middle School in Williamsburg, Virginia is where the life-long friendship was cemented. From that point forward it was rare to not see us together. On the football field was also our first experience working together on a team. It was a football team, but it set the tone and foundation for decades worth of collaborations.

Over the years, our collaborations have hinged on us leveraging each other's strengths and having the autonomy to lead in our respective areas of strength. Even with football, PJ played offense (running back), and I played defensive (linebacker) so we had things covered on both sides of the ball. I relied on PJ to not only play his position but also to lead the offense. He had to be the player and mini coach that could motivate and rally the offense. PJ expected the same thing from me on defense. We remember clearly that our coaches would always tell us, particularly on defense, to play your position and trust your teammate to play theirs – do not try to compensate for your teammate because it causes a break down in the system. These words really stuck, and we have taken that same idea and organically implemented it into all our endeavors. The impressive part is that we have been able to do this for almost 30 years, so this is a concept that has withstood the test of time, we know that it works! We know each other's strengths, weaknesses, pain points and quirks which makes it easier to alter and adjust approaches without reducing our momentum or disturbing our productivity.

This book is a joint project and readers can expect to receive our perspective on conducting business with friends/family. This book can be utilized in several ways.

1) A preparatory tool to be read before entering a business relationship with friends/family.

2) As a handbook or reference manual as you grow your healthy friend/family business relationship.

3) As a tool to assist with the mediation, arbitration and method for addressing current and perceived future issues.

4) It is our business card if you need assistance with any of the concepts mentioned in the book. We are here to assist. You can visit our website www.friendsinbiz.com, or our social media platforms

Facebook Friendsinbiz, Instagram:@Friendsinbiz or simply email us at info@Friendsinbiz.com.

This is a perfect time to provide you all with our credentials so that you might better understand our frame of reference collectively as you read and reference this book.

COLLECTIVELY WE HAVE:

35 years of leadership experience

20k plus hours of advising and coaching

25 years of business experience

22 years of training

15 years of management experiences

3 college degrees

310 hours' worth of college credit

CHAPTER 1:

IS THIS FRIEND THE ONE?

"When you choose your friends, don't be short-changed by choosing personality over character."
- W. Somerset Maugham

When trying to determine if your friend or family member is a good business partner, it is going to require you to set a core criterion that identifies the most important traits that you desire in a business partner. Hopefully, at the top of your list of criteria for entering a business relationship with family/friends regardless of the arrangement, is **TRUST**. 1) Can I trust them? 2) If we are using technical corporate language, are they ethical? We have come to realize for us this is very high on our criteria list, particularly if the financial investment is significant. This should be easy if you are considering a friend or family member and is likely the most appealing factor around doing business with friends and family. You know them, they know you and you all trust each other. However, ethics is only a baseline for trust.

Webster defines Trust as a firm belief in the reliability, truth, ability or strength of something or someone. Trust is something that is developed over time or with the intensity or severity of situations. Trust is like a bank. When you do things to build trust you make a positive deposit. However, when you do things to damage the trust you are making a negative withdrawal. You want to make sure your bank account balance is in good standing - if you want to do business. This is both the gift and the curse of doing business with friends or family. When you enter a business relationship with a loved one, a breakdown in the business as a result of the preexisting friendship equates to a breakdown in the relationship. And remember this relationship is powered by trust. As cliché as it sounds and as much as some readers are going to hate hearing this – it's true. These relationships will always carry with them remnants of this statement "It is not just business it's personal". You cannot fully prevent this from happening. We do not even recommend trying to figure out why. Just know that it is, develop a plan and govern yourselves accordingly. It is all about reducing the potential negative impacts of this type of scenario.

We recommend that you start with the **Friends 1ˢᵗ Business 2ⁿᵈ agreement.** This agreement can be found on our website friendsinbiz.com. We recommend that you do this with a third party in the same way that an engaged couple would go through premarital counseling. This third party does need to understand what they are doing. Our company can facilitate this exercise. This is so important because it provides you all an opportunity at the onset to make plans and enact policies for every situation you can think about or that might be a source of conflict and confusion before the policy is even needed. This is a document that you can have reviewed by a lawyer or that you can have notarized to make it official. You can also revisit it and amend it if needed. This models the concept of being proactive as opposed to reactive. It is like preparing your house for the rain while the sun is still out. That way, when the rain comes, you will be prepared. You all should be in a good place - mind, body and soul, your best selves when constructing this document. The idea is that when this document is needed it can bring you all back to that good place. The place you were in when the document was crafted. This is a great way to keep you all grounded and accountable to each other and to the original plan.

Ok, so trust is the number one quality that makes friend/family endeavors appealing. However, the trust will not stand alone. In the same way, some say love alone will not make a marriage work. Trust is a highly important quality, but it is also largely a feel-good trait. Many things feel good that do not function well. You cannot build a successful and thriving business on trusting a person alone, so allow us to introduce and define some additional qualities that we have found to be preferable and central for entering friend/family enterprises.

Mindset: Establish a set of attitudes that include above-average work ethic, a visionary thought process, positive and optimistic disposition, out of the box thinking and always learning. Mindset is so essential that we have a whole chapter dedicated to it.

Common Sense: Good sense and sound judgment in practical matters. People who can make level-headed socially acceptable comments and decisions that represent the individual and the enterprise in a positive light.

Empathy: The ability to understand and share the feelings of another. Individuals who can show genuine care for people and their situation and are willing to spend time addressing those situations before moving forward with the business.

Self-awareness: Conscious knowledge of one's character, feelings, motives, and desires. Include individuals who have a decent grasp on where they are in life, what their strengths and weaknesses are, what people appreciate about them and how they add value.

When considering which friend(s) are potential business partners, you must make a decision that is both logical and practical. The above are the desired traits that we use as our initial criteria for opting into a business relationship with anybody. Friends and family are not exempt. Let's be clear... they are different! There is the propensity when dealing with a friend or family member to convince yourself that they possess traits that they don't or to inflate the extent to which they possess a trait ranking them with a higher level of proficiency. This is an act of nepotism. If you are not familiar with nepotism, it is the practice among those with the power of influence of favoring relatives or friends, especially by giving them jobs or opportunities. This is an authentic subconscious reflex. However, knowing this we must be hyper-aware as we work to objectively assess our friends and family as business partners.

Here is an example of the type of scenario that most people fear. One of my business acquaintances recently hired one of her family members. She hired the family member purely because they were family. In this situation, I believe there may have even been some family pressure. The family member was grossly underqualified for the job and was frankly a business liability. Not only that but the family member also had some work ethic and character flaws. They were a bit on the lazy side, had a sense of entitlement and attempted to leverage their familiarity as family members with the owner.

Now the owner has an employee that she would have typically never hired who is causing ripples in her normally smooth-running business. This employee is her family member so there are some external family pressures making this work issue a personal issue. The hired family member has a job they would never apply to because it is apparent that they do not qualify, and they are performing in a manner that they typically would not - if they were expected to keep the job. The situation is causing the owner and her employees undo stress.

This example and stories like it are exactly why you must be honest with yourself. It is going to be necessary for addressing shortcomings appropriately if you do decide to move forward with the friend/family business relationship despite some trait reservations. You know there are going to be people that will find a reason to do business with their friend/family despite all the precise and spot-on information given in this book. It is possible that if it is decided to move forward in this fashion that the business relationship can still be successful - but proceed with caution! At least if you are even remotely considering them as a business partner at the minimum you TRUST them.

Outside of the trust quotient, if your family/friend does not fit your other criteria traits there is a chance that your friend fits or fulfills another type of function in the organization. Of course, this can differ vastly based on the enterprise. But they could have a skill set, resources (money) or bring another unique value proposition to the table that may still make the partnership workable or desirable. This may require a restructuring of the business agreement and operations, but hey, at least they are involved and are bringing true value to the project.

Let's dive a bit deeper into this concept of selecting the right friend/family business partner based on core traits. Realize that you are a different person with different life experiences, different ideologies, values, strengths, and gifts. You will need to use what you know about yourself to decide what your desired traits for a business partner should be. Keep in mind, we are still discussing only the core traits. This does not include their gifts, skill sets or influence. As you mature, evolve and even unlearn incorrect, biased or antiquated information or ways of thinking, your perspective of the traits you desire may change or may not change depending on the version of you that is reading this book. We mention that because this would not have been our initial list of traits for a business partner. This list is a result of what life has taught us through trial by error. Thus, this is an opportunity to get you in front of the power curve. You do not have to try and fail as much as we did. We are providing you with the blueprint. That is why you continue to educate yourself and seek self-development. It is the same reason, hopefully, you are reading this book!

When developing your trait criteria list, we recommend thinking in crisis prevention mode. What is the worst thing that can happen if we move forward with this endeavor and what does it have the potential to do to the relationship? What type of core traits do you want in a business partner when things get hard and tough decisions must be made? We personally do not see our core traits changing. Any changes would consist of adding additional traits that we discover as we evolve and as the world around us changes. But it would not include removing the spirit of any of the existing core traits.

How do you determine if the business relationship will damage the relationship? Well if they do not fit your initial criteria, there is a reason to be concerned. If you feel that they will allow the familiarity of the friendship to cause them to make decisions that they would not otherwise make they are also not a good choice. To be honest, you need to survey all their weaknesses to see if you will be resentful if those weaknesses surface in the business relationship.

SIDE NOTE: Do not overly involve other family members, friends or significant others in your business issues, because when you work your issues out, those individuals will still hold on to the emotion that you spoke in when you relayed the issue to them - just like a marriage. Also, never disparage your business partner. If you need to vent, find one individual - a mentor or a confidant (they should possess your core traits) - and that person gets to be your sounding board. Also, introduce the talks that you will have with this person as a venting session or call it whatever you would in your natural lingo. You just want to make them aware that you are venting so that they will not take what you are saying too literally.

"A fool gives full vent to his anger, but a wise man keeps
himself under control"
– Proverbs 29:11

WHAT IS YOUR CORE CRITERIA?

A PERSONAL NOTE ABOUT OUR BUSINESS RELATIONSHIP

One of the things that PJ and I enjoy when it comes to doing business together is that we keep each other humble. We knew each other when we had nothing but love to give to one another. Many of our acquaintances took other less favorable paths in life. Hypothetically speaking, that could have been either one of us. So if anything, we have grown together into the men we are today. This strengthens the business relationship because it is a real friendship. Our connection was not formed through a linking in college because we both shared the same interest or because PJ was good at marketing and I was good at accounting – not that there's anything wrong with that. However, our relationship is significantly more substantive than that. We believe if you have starved with us you have certainly earned an opportunity to eat with us. The derivative benefit there is if one of our endeavors does not yield the expected results or fails, it's ok! We have the core traits, we have starved together before, so we will find a way to eat together again. You must know in your very being and understand clearly that businesses will start, and they will fail. There will be ups in business and downs in business. True friendships and family relationships should remain forever, through the ebbs and flows that happen in the life of a business.

ASSESSING/TESTING THE BUSINESS RELATIONSHIP

The way to measure the integrity of the business decisions that you are making when in business with friends and family is to constantly ask yourself, "Would you make the same decision if there was no personal relationship involved?" This must become a part of your core decision-making process. This can be the first question you ask yourself or the last question, but you must ask the question every time a decision needs to be made. The more important the decision, the longer you should deliberate over it. However, if you are deliberating too long you are likely giving more energy to friendship than the business.

Other factors that should be considered as a part of your decision-making process include asking some of the more standard business questions such as:

1) What's the potential cost of deciding and the potential benefit of making the decision (Cost-Benefit Analysis)? How does what I am preparing to risk (money, credit, credibility, etc.) by entering this endeavor measure up against what I stand to gain, over time?

2) What is the state of the enterprise? Is this decision being made from a place of desperation or is it a calculated, well thought out decision? Is this decision one that is being made under some type of pressure or is this a decision being made with a conscious, sober and sound mind?

Other important questions can and should be asked. What those questions should be will depend on the type of enterprise/organization, the knowledge and business acumen of those individuals involved and the existing relationship. This is a good time to note that there can be a significant risk attached to making business decisions based on personal relationships. In our experience, we have seen this result in one of two different outcomes, possibly both.

•Stifling the growth of the enterprise. Never allowing it to reach its full potential.

•Killing the enterprise and likely the relationship along with it.

RENELDO RANDALL & PJ PIGGOTT

NOTES/ACTIONABLE ITEMS

FRIENDS IN BUSINESS

CHAPTER 2:

VISION CASTING

"Where there is no vision the people perish"

- Proverbs 29:18 KJV

Vision Casting is defined in this context as creating a plan for the future of the enterprise. First let us discuss the relationship between vision and fear. They are two sides of the same coin. People will often not move forward with a vision that they have because of fear and yet fear is a part of the process. In fact, I have heard it said that if your goals and vision do not scare you or evoke fear, then they are not big enough!

When entering into a partnership with a loved one (friend or family member), forming a vision that all parties authentically agree to follow and subscribe to can be a challenging task to navigate. We have found that there are typically two core scenarios that arise:

SCENARIO #1

Friend A brings an idea to Friend B and others. The idea could be, and likely is, tied to their vision or a passion of theirs, which means they are emotionally vested. This makes the joint venture a bit more complex because it could be an idea that other involved parties (Friends and Family) simply see as an okay opportunity but could easily go with another idea.

SCENARIO #2

This includes two or more loved ones deliberating over multiple ideas and finally agreeing collectively that one idea is the most feasible for the group with the skills and resources they have at their disposal.

In scenario #1 when Friend A brings an idea to Friend B and others, Friend B and others need to first ensure that Friend A meets their Friends in Business Partnership Criteria. The next thing Friend B and others need to do is assess how emotionally vested Friend A is in the idea. Note: If you did not write down your Friends in Business Partnership Criteria, now is your opportunity to do so or update it if need be. This criterion is important to the process regardless of where you are in the enterprise relationship (just starting, in the middle or even if considering ending the business relationship).

The concern here for Friend B and others is that Friend A's idea is likely so closely aligned to their personal vision that they may not be so open to receiving feedback, which makes it difficult to form a partnership and, quite frankly, makes it difficult to produce or present the best body of work. You must workshop your ideas in a partnership. But that type of critique can be difficult to receive for someone who is overly vested because it is their "baby." The idea of receiving feedback can decrease substantially if Friend A has low emotional intelligence. Emotional intelligence is defined as the capacity to be aware of, control, and express one's emotions, and to handle interpersonal relationships judiciously and empathetically. Emotional intelligence is an important skill set to have whenever you are working with people, but you will need a double dose when working with family and friends.

Scenario #1 can and has led to successful operations. Communication in this type of scenario is paramount. Friend A needs to articulate their vision the best they can but be open to workshopping the idea with the team to develop the best version of the idea. Friend B and others need to ensure that they have all their concerns addressed thoroughly enough and feel comfortable moving forward with the next steps. Lastly, Friend A must be content with the fact that their idea may not be the best idea at that time.

Scenario #2, in our opinion, requires less brain power in terms of trying to think through the partnership process, the autonomy of the vision and the pitch. This is because the group is discussing with individuals they trust and, hopefully, have most of the other qualities they need and desire in business partners. Otherwise, you all should not even be sitting at the table together discussing business anyway - at least not seriously. The keyword in Scenario #2 that differentiates it from Scenario #1 is "discussion". Let's just call this a brainstorming session. This differs from scenario #1 where an idea was brought to the group.

In this scenario because the trust is established, to whatever extent, one can discuss their vision or other viable business ideas. Therefore, it's an opportunity for a member of the group to present an idea that they feel passionate about and receive feedback in a safe place because there is no expectation for immediate buy-in and everyone should be open to and expecting feedback. Ultimately, a team will need to be formed and if potential team members are not onboard for valid, or substantial enough reasons, then the idea may need work or it may not be the right time and on occasion, you might be with the wrong group. At the end of the day, during the brainstorming discussion, the best idea should prevail.

In Scenario #2 type environments it is much easier to agree on a shared vision naturally. The action steps on how to move forward with the vision may require research but the vision is established. There will be necessary future discussions that will happen as the due diligence process is carried out and changes should be expected. However, everyone is on the same page and can always return to the vision as a point of reference and clarity.

WHERE DO WE SEE THE BUSINESS GOING?

A question that comes up frequently or eventually is "Where do we see the business going?", which is the vision for the business. So a better question would be, "Where do you see the business going next?" If the enterprise is profitable (operating in the black) then things are going well. If in this position, because businesses must always be looking towards the future, owners should be asking themselves questions such as, "Should we grow to expand and if so, how and how quickly?", "Should we diversify if so in what ways?" and/or "Should we give pay increases and if so, how much?" Operating in the black and being profitable and/or having an operation that is running smoothly is the optimal space to be in. Yet, there is always pressure to remain in that position. Especially, since the reality is that, on average, most small businesses are not profitable or will fail in the first 3 to 5 years.

Everyone has their reasons for why they would select one option over another. Much of that should be driven by profit and/or productivity of the operation. This creates an opportunity for continuous conversation between friends/family in the business. You all are certainly aware of each other's personal reasons for favoring some decisions over others. This could impact the business friendship positively or negatively. The most realistic way to cope with a decision that you did not favor is to ensure that there is a reasonable compromise and setting a date to assess outcomes.

Let us give you a tangible example. We are investors in a spa and salon. A decision was made to provide pay increases to some of the staff. Initially, we did not feel this was a prudent decision. The rationale was given that a raise was provided because they are dedicated staff who keep the operation running and it was a tangible way of showing gratitude. This is a decision that we agreed to because the concept made sense although the revenue did not necessarily support it. If we were not friends with the majority owners, this may not have been something that we would have entertained. The reasonable compromise was that we later developed a strategy for increasing the cost of services.

We feel it necessary to mention that when you are making wise and profitable business decisions with friends/family, it is an amazing experience. The combination of a leisure relationship plus a business relationship with people you know, love and trust is bliss! However, business has its ups and downs, so the strategy is to expect the best and plan for the worst.

WHAT ARE OUR ROLES?

Roles and responsibilities are another hot button topic in friend/family business operations. As the enterprise grows and evolves it makes sense for roles and responsibilities to change and, in most cases, it's necessary for the operation to grow. We have often heard pastors talk about the church startup experience and how the founding members did everything. The pastor could help park the cars, preach the sermon, sing the opening selection, read the announcements and then clean the bathrooms after service. The first lady did the books. The deacons and deaconesses did everything else from offering, audio visual to maintenance. They just went to work. But as the church grew and their membership grew the church added to the congregation individuals that had certain knowledge, skills, and abilities who were more capable and more qualified or who were equally capable and qualified but who had more time. At that point, that added to their resource pool. It made sense to release, adjust and reassign certain duties, roles, and expectations. This can be a point of contention, especially among smaller organizations that were initially established with friends/family when someone is no longer the right person for the job. It's not an exaggeration to say that there will be family/friends who feel like they should be in roles that they are neither prepared nor qualified for.

Everyone must be on the same page about what growth means and what it could look and feel like. This type of communication is paramount, and it is important to establish it early and exercise it as often as needed. Make sure to do this while always keeping the mission at the forefront and referring to the vision as a consultant and as a barometer to every change.

NOTES/ACTIONABLE ITEMS

CHAPTER 3:

COMMUNICATION

"The single biggest problem in communication is the illusion that it has taken place."

\- George Bernard Shaw

Communication is important in any relationship. Lack of communication or unclear communications is third on the list of reasons marriages end only preceded by infidelity and money. These relationship rules cross over from marriage into friendships and business enterprises. Essentially, infidelity (trust) and money affect relationships. We have already addressed trust and will speak about money but felt that communication should come before money in this book because if you can get the communication right and keep it tight perhaps there will not be money issues and just fewer issues in general.

CONSTRUCTIVE CRITICISM

Let's start with constructive criticism since this is necessary for business but often difficult to receive from family and friends, especially if it is not delivered correctly. The standard definition for constructive criticism is the process of offering valid and well-reasoned opinions about the work of others, usually involving both positive and negative comments, in a friendly manner rather than an oppositional one.

Ok, so in any healthy friendship, there should be an expectation of accountability. Your friend should have your best interest in mind and not let you do anything unwise or out of character. Examples of unwise decisions could include things as simple as wearing a distasteful outfit or posting something inappropriate on social media.

You would assume this concept would transfer over into the business relationship seamlessly. However, accountability and the expectations of accountability are not always handled appropriately. Let's address why this might be the case. We believe that there are two reasons this happens:

1) The core friendship has issues that need to be addressed before they think about partnering in business.

2) Providing constructive criticism, constructively, is just hard.

It's a difficult skill set to develop and if you do, it's rare that your feedback is received the way you intended. The initial words that you string together and the awkwardness that comes along with you needing to have the conversation requires time to get comfortable with. This process is difficult by its very nature. If you are not careful and intentional about being prepared your reflex is to avoid the uncomfortable conversation because you fear the conflict. Falling into this trap extinguishes accountability. Typically, whatever needs to be addressed doesn't just go away... it still needs to be addressed. Without addressing the issue, you are allowing it to fester, build and intensify until a point of frustration.

Here is where the lack of communication becomes apparent because this whole scenario can take place without the 2nd party - the person who should have received the constructive criticism - even knowing.

This is a clear example of what happens when there are communication breakdowns. The frustration that one party is experiencing may not even be on the 2nd parties' radar. Yet the 1st party is showing in various ways, some voluntary and some non-voluntary, that they are frustrated. The other parties may or may not feel or witness this frustration. If they do feel or witness it, they are not sure what's causing this change in behavior. They may inquire about the change in behavior. They may just decide to deal with the 1st party in the same way that the 1st party is dealing with them or again the 2nd party may not even notice the frustration. As you can see this can cause unnecessary complexity and confusion. That is why we are firm believers that providing feedback through constructive criticism is a valuable communication channel when exercised appropriately. However, this is done best and easiest when there is an understanding and a culture that supports such actions. Completing the Friends 1st Business 2nd Agreement gets you in front of situations like this and establishes a culture conducive to open, honest and on time communication.

PJ has always said, "We are the same person" and without him explaining to me exactly what he meant I have always understood him to mean that because we share many of the same experiences, have shared in each other's experiences, and have developed a common way of thinking that we were "the same". However, as we have gotten older it's become apparent that we are still very different which makes for richer and more well-rounded conversations. We do however still share a similar way of thinking which makes for productive communication. We have known each other for so long and know each other so well that we understand each other on a deeper level. This has created a competitive advantage for us because we, without a conversation, learned how to leverage it positively. It helps us give and receive constructive criticism and feedback without having to put the same time, thought and effort into the process.

Thus, we are not the same person, but we are two sides of the same coin, two parts make the whole. With age comes wisdom, and as we have gotten older, we have become more intentional about identifying our differences or our different strengths and utilizing them. It's because we understand each other, respect each other, and know that we have each other's best interest in mind that makes it easier for us to give each other constructive criticism and for the other to accept it. We are now at the point where we expect and ask for constructive criticism because we desire to get better. We are too busy being productive to be sensitive about the feedback.

So let's discuss how to make your criticisms constructive starting out. It boils down to 3 things: timing, language, and history.

1) **Timing:** You must make sure you bring up your concerns with them at an opportune time. If you know they are not a morning person do not talk to them about it in the morning. They need to be in a good state of mind and so do you.

2) **Language:** You need to make sure you introduce the criticism with the right words and use the right words throughout the conversation. Do not use accusatory words or statements. Try to stay away from using the word YOU. Example "You did not pay the bill." Instead, you can ask. "What happened with the bill payment?"

3) **History:** You want to have a good history of productive conversations. If that history is not there, you will want to start to build it. People will typically handle you how they have always handled you in the past. If you have always had aggressive conversations this is what they will expect, so you must change that culture.

We will be honest, this takes practice. If you need to expedite this process you can bring in a 3rd party mediator or use a common unbiased friend that you feel might be better equipped to deliver the news. We have used 3rd party friends on occasions but please be advised you must get the right individual. If you chose the wrong person, it could make things worse.

Over the last 30 years, we have done a good job of mastering each other. This, of course, was a process. However, now that we understand the power of it and have intentionally discussed it, we can now strategically control this asset by gaining an even deeper understanding of each other's strengths and weaknesses and maximizing them. Thus, we have gotten into the practice of taking personality tests and strength inventories to see how closely they align with what we already thought about ourselves. It was interesting to see how our strengths, weaknesses, and commonalities played off each other. It helped us to confirm our behaviors and tweak or at least be at peace concerning how we operate.

We strongly recommend that you do this with your team. This can assist your team with uncovering some of the frustrations that you all may be having with one another or identify some of the traits that may be going unrecognized. Highlighting the strengths, weaknesses, and commonalities aids in starting healthy conversations concerning individual and team improvements as well as shifting roles and responsibilities backed by third party evidence. Therefore, it is not simply one person's opinion. We do recommend that you take several of these assessments to help provide more validation of this self-discovery. We have included a few free assessments that we have used.

High5 Test: https://high5test.com/ (free Strengths test that has helped +7500,000 people)

16Personalities: https://www.16personalities.com/free-personality-test (Free Personality Test)

Enneagram: https://www.truity.com/test/enneagram-personality-test (From one point of view, the **Enneagram** can be seen as a set of nine distinct **personality** types. Each number on the **Enneagram** denoting one type. It is common to find a little of yourself in all nine of the types, although; one of them should stand out as being closest to yourself.)

WHAT DID YOU DISCOVER ABOUT YOURSELF AND THE MEMBERS OF YOUR TEAM AFTER COMPLETING THE ASSESSMENT(S)?

HOW TO FIGHT AGAINST JEALOUSY AND ENVY

Jealousy and envy can ruin anything! It's been argued that jealousy is normal. If this is true, then it makes what's covered in this section that much more important. You must keep telling yourself, as long as everyone is pulling their weight, it is a team effort. Then you really must make sure the pulling of the weight is equal according to everyone's area of strength. It may be that your area of strength puts you behind the scenes and the other partner(s) are the face of the operation. If you are bothered by this, don't be prideful. Find an opportunity to mention how you are feeling. It may present itself as criticism so be mindful of the timing, language, and history.

In general, you should make a concerted effort to ensure that recognition is distributed equally. No man or woman is an island and has become successful by themselves. Whatever the endeavor is, it's a team sport. If I can use a sports analogy-Michael Jordan is regarded as the best basketball player of all time, by many. However, he could not win one game let alone 6 championships without assistance. It took a team of people playing their position to make that happen. Make sure that everyone feels appreciated and respected for their contribution. This will require you to be purposeful about showing genuine appreciation and to be observant of the needs and temperaments of your team. You should be aware of how your personality affects others. This is another opportunity for you to utilize personality tests and strength inventories to familiarize yourself with the type of people on your team such as: how they work, what their strengths are, what they need in order to be successful and what they need to remain productive and engaged. This will again help with limiting the number conflicts and fostering a better understanding of others on the team.

HOW TO MAINTAIN A FRIENDSHIP OUTSIDE OF THE BUSINESS RELATIONSHIP

Maintaining the friendship outside of the business means to continue to do the things that you enjoyed as friends before you were business partners. For us this happened organically. We just enjoy fellowshipping with like-minded friends, discussing big ideas and helping people. It's healthy to get together and enjoy each other's company without discussing business. It allows you to enjoy one another outside of the enterprise. Prayerfully, it will also keep you grounded and focused on what is most important and that is the ones you love and your relationship. World-renowned speaker, singer, author and media personality, Dr. Willie Jolly said that "We are jugglers and all the balls we juggle are rubber, that is they all bounce back, except for one. One of them is glass, and not only glass but very fine Tiffany glass. This ball represents your family/friends and that is the only ball that will break on contact." Always keep your eye and hand on that ball.

FREQUENCY OF COMMUNICATION, THE TYPE OF COMMUNICATION AND WHEN TO USE IT

In business, you will be in constant communication with your partners and staff. Much of this communication is likely to happen via various electronic mediums simply because phone conversations are hard to arrange with busy people. They are also becoming less necessary for quick questions and responses to time-sensitive questions. An electronic message on the run is very efficient in these cases. Therefore, you and your partners must understand each other well. Your understanding should be to the point that you can translate, decode and discern what they may mean when sending you a message via e-mail, text, instant messenger or direct message that may seem cryptic or short. By knowing your partners and giving them the benefit of the doubt, understanding their personality and temperament goes a long way. When you are conducting business with a friend, you also want to make sure that you are not neglecting the friendship. This means you must be intentional about making sure they are in a good place. Now, good colleagues, business partners, and leaders should do this anyhow. However, when there is a pre-existing friendship it becomes more important. There is a business reason for this. They are your friend and you have a responsibility to inquire about their wellbeing on a personal level. Hopefully, helping them through problems they might be facing personally will allow them to recover quickly so that they can then focus on the business.

NEVER VENT DOWN ALWAYS VENT UP OR LATERAL

We do want to reiterate here that disagreements will happen even after you have taken the time to complete the Friends 1st Business 2nd agreement, discussed constructive criticism and have taken personality tests and strength inventories. You will disagree. This is natural and necessary for growth, so embrace it.

There will be times when you need to vent before you can come back and communicate effectively. You do not want to vent to anyone that does not have the best interest of all parties in mind. You also do not want to influence how anyone feels about the other party or parties. Best practice would be to vent to someone not directly affiliated or financially tied to the business. In multi-level marketing we say never "vent down". Not venting down essentially means that you should not vent to your subordinates. You want to make sure you are venting to someone who is at a lateral level or higher and who is as unbiased as possible, but mature enough to give sound advice or just provide a confidential listening ear. It's good practice for partners to choose who they would want to be their collective sounding board(s). Having that type of individual in place allows the partners to feel comfortable knowing that they have someone they can confide in.

Partners could agree to utilize the same person. There are obvious benefits with this type of arrangement, as this person would be privy to both parties' issues. We do recommend that you enter your venting session with the disclaimer that you are just venting so that the sounding board person knows exactly how to process and approach what you are sharing with them. This can be important because venting sessions do not always require advice or feedback. The sounding board person needs to know what you expect from them at that moment. If you are seeking advice or feedback you may want to consider consulting a professional.

Please remember after your venting session, particularly if what you were venting about concerns business critical matters, that you will still need to find the right time to start a healthy dialog with your partner(s).

NOTES/ACTIONABLE ITEMS

FRIENDS IN BUSINESS

CHAPTER 4:

MONEY MATTERS

"Money Does Not Change Men, it Merely Unmasks Them"
- Henry Ford

We don't feel we are surprising anyone by saying that money is a touchy subject in any type of relationship. We have already identified money as being number two on the list of reasons marriages end. It might be the number one reason behind businesses ending between friends and family. Honestly, most people view money as a scarce resource and people are risk-averse by nature. Thus, when it comes to putting their liquid cash, their financial nest egg or their credit on the line they are apprehensive. However, there will be people that are less risk-averse, passionate about the project and believe 200% in the vision – bona fide risk-takers. The two types of people I just described, the risk-averse person and the risk taker, gives context to how these two types of people feel about money - which, in most cases, affects how they invest their money. We could write another book on the variables that go into creating these different types of thought processes and relationships concerning money. I am going to mention just a few of the notable variables that foster these different schools of thought concerning money, spending, and investing.

Notable variables would include:

•Partners' past relationship with money. If there are partners who have never been in possession of much money, they could be leery about spending it or investing it.

•How partners view money currently. If they are experiencing financial issues or have other personal plans that require their resources.

•Consider the responsibilities of each partner involved in the building of the enterprise.

Unequal distribution of responsibilities has the potential to create a significant impact in family life and family makeup. For example, if there are partners who are married with children vs. partners who are single, divorced or have no children. Generally speaking, a single person has the freedom to move about differently, as they are only responsible for themselves. Where a married person is accountable to their spouse and responsible for their children - if they have any. PJ and I have this dynamic. Currently, I have been married for 11 years and have three kids (ages 21, 9 and 4) and PJ is single with no kids.

Please note that when in business and considering these variables you must remain mindful that things are not always created equal and that the dynamics can be interesting. Equal giving of time, talent and treasure (money) does not necessarily mean equal sacrifice - figure out a way to make it equitable. Also important is how much one believes in the project, the capabilities of the team, the planning, the overall vision and its sustainability.

NOTE: In a perfect world the team should endeavor to strike a balance between the risk-taker and the risk averse. Let's call that strategic risk-taking. If you are unsure how to assess a strategic risk visit www.friendsinbiz.com and download the Strategic Risk Assessment Tool.

DISCUSSION ABOUT MONEY, DECISIONS ABOUT MONEY

Understanding the two ends of the risk continuum is important when discussing money and money decisions. Topics include investment, reinvestment, credit, profits, losses, etc. It is always wise to have a conversation about these money topics when all involved parties are in a good state of mind and thinking both intelligently and objectively. This is a conversation that needs to be had before money problems arise. You never want to make decisions while you are in a state of crisis. You can never quite see or think clearly in crisis mode. A state of crisis can be likened to a storm. When you are driving in a storm you make all types of adjustments that alter the way you normally drive. You drive slower, turn on the windshield wipers, the defrost, turn down the radio, turn on the flashers, etc. You do not need or want that type of pressure when making financial decisions. You should do your best to thoroughly address any and every potential business area and type of issue that might arise. This will make discussions about money go much smoother. You should also revisit the Strategic Risk Assessment tool as needed to update it, when the team is in a good state of mind, and ready and able to make intelligent and optimistic decisions. This document should be reviewed annually. We recommend reviewing this document during an annual strategic planning meeting.

FULL TRANSPARENCY CONCERNING MONEY

What does full transparency mean? It means being completely up-front and honest. In our opinion there are 3 different levels of honesty: Basic Honesty, Honesty 2.0 and Full Disclosure.

1) **Basic Honesty:** This is the first level of honesty as most dictionaries define it. At this level, people will provide the information that is asked of them simply and truthfully providing nothing more or nothing less. They do this even when they know or feel that providing more context to the response is needed. The context in this case is enough to change the way the information is received or perceived.

2) **Honesty 2.0:** This is where people will provide the necessary (needed) additional content that is absent in first level - basic honesty. Here is where you hope to receive historical sentiments, professional observations/opinions, and collaborative feedback.

3) **Full Disclosure:** The third and last level of honesty. At this level you share everything. Nothing is off-limits.

Full Transparency is a must when it comes to money. We have already established the different relationships people have with money. Particularly, our risk-averse partners out there. You must exercise level 3 honesty "Full Disclosure" and learn how to make your approach natural and comfortable enough for you and your partner(s). This should become the normal expectation. This full transparency and full disclosure must happen in order to establish and maintain trust. Once the trust is broken regarding money, partners begin to lose their fidelity towards other partners and their zeal towards the enterprise.

TRUST CONCERNING MONEY

If you don't trust members of the team with your money or with the ability to produce a needed investment, then you probably should not be doing business with them period - because there is no TRUST. Trust is the first quality we address when considering a business partner. You may choose to move forward with a business relationship even in the absence of trust; I can see this happening if a partner has a business-critical skill that you need. Then you might reluctantly consider doing business with them. But it is recommended that you set up clear lines of communication, expectations and terms of the agreement. You will want to add items to the agreement such as reasonable deadlines, two signature approval, contracts with clear language concerning ownership distribution, detailed and clear job descriptions, buyout protocol and dissolution protocols.

For PJ and I, this is where our unique friendship and humble beginnings become a formal part of our business lives. Our first formal business entity was a non-profit organization Real People Educating Others (rpeova.org). We entered this world of entrepreneurship and business as servants and social entrepreneurs. As a small non-profit with no real cash flow, we funded almost everything. 90% of anything we did was paid for by us, so money and receiving payment for our services was not the driving force and was never anything that we focused on. We not only shared our personal money but we often pooled money and gave it away to those in need. When you have people with giving and sacrificial spirits like that as a part of your core team it makes conversation about money easier to have.

When we finally generated some funding for our non-profit, it was not difficult to budget and appropriate funds. We were good stewards over little, so we are better stewards over much.

In the multi-level marketing/direct sales space, the way the compensation plan was structured, the "Upline", who is the individual who introduces or recruits a person into the business (in this case PJ) is not successful unless the "downline" - the individual being recruited into the business (in this case me) is successful. The company's organizational structure and compensation plan was designed to keep us accountable to each other and tied our income generating abilities to each other.

As investors in the Spa and Salon industry, we had to produce liquid cash to cover unexpected expenses, advance payroll, and cover rent and equipment lease payments. These are things that were not contractually our responsibility. However, we knew that we either pay now or we pay later. We believed in the potential of the business, so we split the responsibility and liability. We have used this same philosophy and divide and conquer attitude when approaching other strategic partnerships.

When you are able to grow in business as friends and maintain a solid friendship, you find ways to create win-win scenarios, develop a clear focus and learn to have open communication about money. At the end of the day, everyone is in business to make money. However, there will be times when money is lost. During these periods, you should still have the reassurance of knowing that you all will work through the issues together.

RESISTING GREED

This philosophy also works when addressing greed. You must trust the members of your team, invest back into the business and split the profit fairly. Equitable splitting of the profits is usually comparable to the initial investment by each partner. If one partner invests 70% and the other invests 30%, then the revenue split on the back end should resemble the investment on the front end unless other arrangements have been made between the parties. You do want to be cautious because there can be resentment if one or more partners feel that their investment does not fairly reflect in their return on investment.

For example, you don't want the individual who is investing 70% and the individual who is investing 30% to have a 50/50 revenue split, simply because they are friends. Make the investment to revenue split equitable for long term growth. The group can define what is fair based on what each partner is bringing to the venture, as well as the amount of risk each partner is assuming. In the past, we have both invested in a business where we have taken on too much financial risk and have had more hands-on involvement in the business than our profit split agreement required of us. Admittedly, if we had not been doing business with friends, we would have conducted business differently.

That is why we recommend contributing financially equally and fairly or in other valuable ways (i.e. supplying a special skill, industry knowledge, significant connections, etc.) that are congruent with standard business practice and protocols. Likewise, partners should accept and agree on profit splits that are in line with investments, associated risk and the longevity of the enterprise unless otherwise agreed upon and documented.

NOTES/ACTIONABLE ITEMS

FRIENDS IN BUSINESS

CHAPTER 5:

MINDSET

"If you change the way you look at things, the things you look at change."

- Wayne Dyer

People come from different walks of life, but what connects us is our belief systems, shared experiences, and other commonalities. These are the same areas that develop our ideologies and, ultimately, form our mindset. Typically, having a business or entrepreneurial mindset means that you think strategically about the activities and ventures that you take part in. You don't just go to any networking event, take on any job or partner on every project. You are the type of person who has an idea of what decisions can mean both short-term and long-term before you invest your time, talent, or treasures.

At an early age, we understood that we wanted to be successful. With the experience that we had at that time we felt that to become successful we had to: 1) complete college and 2) obtain well-paying careers. This is what we witnessed those that came before us do to elevate themselves to the same or similar level of accomplishment we hoped to achieve. We also wanted to be men of influence and it seemed reasonable that finishing college and getting good jobs would put us on a trajectory towards achieving that goal. Completing college or some type of formal training and getting a good job is a normal path to the middle-class lifestyle. However, this path is not typically designed to create the type of mindset that laid dormant in us. The mindset that we were not taught in school and that was awakened in us after we graduated from college and started our careers. The mindset that caused us to want to be men of influence and have above average lifestyles.

It was at that point we realized that a college degree or its equivalent, and subsequent good career would not get us the influence and lifestyle we desired. College equipped us well to start careers and to adopt comfortable middle-class lifestyles. It afforded us all the things we needed and many of the things we wanted. All that was required is that we go to work and work hard. Then in return, we could come home to enjoy some leisure-time, hopefully, have a little discretionary income and live a simple, comfortable and stable life.

There was just a feeling that we both shared of wanting something more. Wanting to have more significance and do more with our lives, that caused us to desire more and that desire gave rise to a different way of thinking. It wasn't something that was developed during any one time in our lives but something that was developed over time and was refined by a series of experiences and exposures. A notable exposure was our involvement in multi-level- marketing/network marketing. Our time in this space helped to rapidly expand our mindsets and the way we viewed the world and money. We began to take inventory of our lives, collectively, recalling the many people we have had the pleasure of meeting, speaking to and working with. Through this exercise we confirmed to ourselves that a person's mindset is everything. From that point on, building our mindsets became a priority.

Napoleon Hill, bestselling author of "Think and Grow Rich" has a famous quote that states, "Whatever the mind can believe, the mind can achieve." To expand the development of our mindsets further than we could see, feel, and touch we sought further exposure through reading, taking classes and attending seminars. We both attended college and paid tuition to receive instruction to complete our degrees. Paying for education was not a foreign concept to us. However, when we first started considering attending seminars, we were a bit reluctant because of the price tags. We were also not accustomed to paying for or attending classes outside of a formal educational institution. We were lucky enough to have some mentors who encouraged us to be lifelong learners and endorsed the idea of attending these types of events. We also heard the same anecdotes echoed in books and in audio programs, so this became a part of our mindset shift. We reasoned that if we did not pay now, we would suffer later. We also began to understand that it takes money to make money. The money that we would pay for what may be thought of as non-traditional education is like obtaining a college degree. It guarantees you nothing. It is simply education and education is a tool. Famous entrepreneur, author, and motivational speaker Jim Rhon articulates the notion of investing in yourself this way, "It isn't what the book costs, it's what it will cost you if you don't read it".

We now attend at least one conference a year to help sharpen our mindsets. We have had the honor of being at conferences with speakers such as Dr. Eric Thomas, Stedman Graham, Tony Robbins, Robert Kiyosaki, and Dr. Willie Jolley, to name a few. They have all assisted us in our personal, business, and family lives. We also take the time to share anything that we are reading or listening to with each other so that we might grow together and discuss how we can make the information applicable to anything that we might have going on during that season in life. After attending many classes, conventions, seminars and reading several books, we are now honored to provide valuable information to others through the same mediums.

In our journey through trial and error, we have discovered that a mindset or certain mode of thinking is not something that you can force onto people. It almost always must be a gentle dripping of information. You must meet people where they are. Remember that the individuals that you will encounter have their own mindset. As mentioned, people are different and are all at different stages in their lives and developments. It's the diversity we enjoy and should embrace as it provides perspective on the larger world. Thus, when building connections with others you must be mindful of their unique differences as you try to see where your respective mindsets might align and as you assess them to see if they are open to receiving new information. This helps to build the relationship and avoid unnecessary and unintentional conflict.

Improving your mindset is a daily commitment. You must be intentional about your mind and be prayerful about your actions. You must remain open-minded and become a good listener. We remember when our mind was not where it is today. We remain open-minded to everything because we never know what information we might receive that could advance our mindset even further. Our motto is that *it does not cost money to listen.*

We motivate and lift each other up through the exchange of quotes, words of encouragement, inspirational videos, and prayer. We have found that this is one way that we have been able to keep each other focused, encouraged, and committed. We've witnessed people start projects that they were excited about only to experience some turbulence or adversity and give up. This is a commitment issue and commitment is a mindset. We like the way the author, keynote speaker, advisor and former publisher of SUCCESS Magazine, Darren Hardy defines commitment. He says commitment is doing the thing you said you were going to do, long after the mood you said it in has left you. People are more prone to give up when things get hard or their plans get derailed as opposed to doubling down and focusing. We understand that to be productive it takes being consistent and comprehending the idea that hard times may occur, but also that it is part of the journey. It's a growing pain. When we decide that it is prudent to move forward on a project and we attach ourselves to it, we are going to make sure that the project gets completed. That is the expectation that we set for each other and it is fortified by our mindset. We realize that developing a mindset that allows you to do business and align and connect can be difficult and takes work.

We have developed a 10 step model for Mindset Acquisition and Maintenance that will assist you with establishing or reviving a mindset that can become your new standard. This is significant information because we must all understand that, fundamentally, your **Mindset Will Supersede Your Skill Sets**.

This concept is proven and is part of the history and fabric of global powerhouses like McDonald's. If you know the story or have seen the movie *The Founder* on Netflix, you will recall the narrative where the McDonald brothers had the skill set and developed the system. However, Ray Crock had the mindset and the vision that ultimately created the billion-dollar global company that we know today.

The first three steps of the Mindset Acquisition and Maintenance Model focus on the acquisition of the appropriate mindset.

1) **Decision:** The first rule is simply making the decision that you want to change your mindset. Once you make this decision you must understand what your "WHY" is. What's pushing you to make this change. Then you must do something tangible, putting some skin in the game so that you are vested in this mindset shift. This can range from making a monetary investment towards the mindset shift to telling trusted friends, confidants or mentors.

2) **Discipline:** You must begin to exercise discipline immediately. I can guarantee you that any successful person you know has systems that they follow and that they are consistently accountable. They are also likely good stewards over their time, talents, and treasures. You will find that they also have accountability partners that can speak with them openly and honestly.

Jim Rohn has a quote that brings color to this idea of discipline. He states that "Discipline weighs ounces and regret weighs tons." This quote speaks volumes to the fact that discipline is uncomfortable and comes with a cost, but it is nothing compared to the cost and discomfort that comes with being undisciplined.

3) **Obsession:** Obsession, in this case, consists of having an idea or thought that continually preoccupies or intrudes on your mind – be obsessive. When your mindset changes people should notice that change. It should be noticeable enough that people comment on it. The comments could be positive, like "She has taken a serious interest in…" or it could be negative "All he talks about is…". Either way it is the recognition that your mind is preoccupied or that you are vested in that thing.

The next seven steps of the Mindset Acquisition and Maintenance model concern maintaining the appropriate mindset.

4) **Personal Development**: You must emerge yourself in positive personal development. We suggest you do this by introducing your subconscious to positivity first thing in the morning as a way of owning your day. The world, unfortunately, feeds you negativity so you need to combat that energy early. Engulf yourself in a mix of motivation and content-rich material.

5) **Self-talk**: This is a natural progression to your personal development because once you have digested this information you should be able to speak it to yourself. This can happen in the form of continually recalling information and applying it to your life using affirmations or incantations. Affirmations are the action or process of affirming something or being affirmed. "I am intelligent, I am worthy, I am capable, etc." Incantations are similarly defined as a series of words said as a magic spell or charm. You are feeding your mind ideas about you. These ideas are going from your lips to your ears. You are speaking life into yourself!

6) **Tighten up your Circle**: Rap artist, Beanie Sigel, in his 2005 song, *Feel It In The Air,* has a line where he says, "Tighten up your circle before they hurt you, read their body language 85% communication non-verbal". The takeaway here is that everyone that you want to go with you is not meant to go into this next stage of life - or at least not into your business venture. This also means that you must be careful not to tell major things to minor people because they cannot always process your big dream – plus it's your dream, not theirs. As you evolve, some people in your current circle may not be ready

for your evolution. They may feel intimidated or uncomfortable by your evolution or simply do not want to be left behind. Your growth shines a light on their stagnation. This can cause them to be cancers. "You are the average of the Five People you spend the most time with" – Jim Rohn

7) **Help People**: You want to help as many people as possible as often as possible. Helping people to get what they want and need, without expecting anything in return, will cause you to win by default. We call this the reciprocity of the atmosphere.

8) **Gratitude**: Gratitude is defined as the quality of being thankful or readiness to show appreciation. You should make it a habit to thank people in a genuine way often.

9) **Be Uncomfortable**: Get comfortable being uncomfortable. You must remember that being uncomfortable is a part of every growth process. The thought of discomfort and uncertainty are intimidating but they are also symbolic of advancement and growth. People are inherently scared of failure but remember success is typically on the other side of failure or fear of failure.

10) **Balance**: Balance is defined as a condition in which different elements are equal or in the correct positions. Steps 1 through 9 are going to put you out of balance and they should because you are working hard to get and keep this new mindset. You'll lose sleep, you may lose friends, your routines will change. However, you had responsibilities before this, and you still must handle those responsibilities. We encourage you to remember your priorities (Faith, Family, and Finances). Additionally, know that you will always be juggling multiple priorities and will constantly have to readjust priorities to keep your life in balance.

NOTES/ACTIONABLE ITEMS

THANK YOU

We would like to thank everyone who supported this book. It truly means a lot to us. We hope that the book helps to ease the anxiety of doing business with family and/or friends. Our mission was to share our journey and along the way provide some of the concepts, thought processes and rules that have allowed us to be successful. We understand that each group's story and relationship is different. However, we are confident that the resources that are shared in this book will be instrumental in the building, rebuilding, and sustainability of your Friends in Business relationship.

These principles are not limited to being in business with family and friends. Many of these principles can be incorporated into your family life, your career, and other business ventures with others (non-friends). The content in this book also transcends business sectors and enterprise types. The book is an appropriate high-utility tool for corporations, non-profits, civic organizations, boards of directors, business schools, business accelerators and incubators, entrepreneurship programs, as well as high school business and marketing programs.

ABOUT THE AUTHORS

RENELDO RANDALL, MBA

Reneldo Randall is a dynamic and savvy authority on successful leadership in advancing human and intellectual capital; a big-picture visionary who understands how daily operations shape results and goals. As a motivated achiever, he is recognized domestically and abroad for combining excellence, integrity, and innovation with best practices and "common sense" to achieve immediate and long-term goals. As a higher education administrator, non-profit leader, business strategist and leadership consultant, he is an effective manager of people with unsurpassed interpersonal skills.

ABOUT THE AUTHORS

PJ PIGGOTT, BS

PJ Piggott, B.S. is a visionary entrepreneur who is revered and respected as a strategic connector of people. A leader who motivates individuals to push past their limits to achieve their goals. A serial entrepreneur who has an eye for business niches as well as an ability to market them effectively. As a healthcare professional, athletic coach, non-profit and top multi-level marketing leader, he is an impressive shepherd of people with an unmatched work ethic.

LET'S GROW TOGETHER

We invite you to join our social media community

FACEBOOK: Friendsinbiz

INSTAGRAM: Friendsinbiz

We also invite you to visit our web page www.friendsinbiz.com to schedule your FREE 20-minute coaching session and join one of our mastermind groups.

Made in the USA
Columbia, SC
21 February 2025